I Always Put My Mouth On Her

A Collection of Affirmations for Women

DR. FREDERICK D. ACKLIN

Copyright © 2021 by Dr. Frederick D. Acklin

All rights reserved. No part of this publication may be reproduced, distributed, or transmitted in any form or by any means, including photocopying, recording, or other electronic or mechanical methods, without the prior written permission of the publisher, except in the case of brief quotations embodied in critical reviews and certain other noncommercial uses permitted by copyright law. For permission requests, write to the publisher, addressed "Attention: Permissions Coordinator," at the address below.

ISBN: 978-1-7346343-5-8

Publishing By:
DemiCo National, LLC
www.DemiCoNational.com

My tongue is a pen of a ready writer.

Psalms 45:1

TABLE of CONTENTS

Forward	9
Introduction	11
Voice Activation	13
Daddy's Girl	15
The Orphan Spirit	19
A Collection of Prayers	21
I Put My Money Where My Mouth Is	25
Effective Communication	29
Love From A Healed Man	33
30 Day Affirmational Challenge	47
It's Okay To Go Down on Her	63

FORWARD

As the writer of *Put Your Mouth on Him*, my book acted as a guiding post for women to exhibit what it takes to be the creator of the climax for the men in their lives. While there appears to be a sexual connotation, the intent is not directed to only married couples, but male-female of all kinds. While it was a surprise, it is also an honor to be given the opportunity to share my thoughts for this masterful work by Dr. Acklin. First, I would like to give homage to Dr. Acklin for having the courage and audacity to tackle such a vital topic.

In my opinion, the man was designed with a uniqueness which differs from women. Men are revered as the Priest, Protector and Provider, by MOST women. They look to rescue us, they are not very emotional, well most of them are not very emotional. I pray that this book allows men to explore this delicate, yet essential example of proper use of the tongue to help them create a reservoir of life. I believe the culture of our community as we have known it has taken a position of silence as it relates to cultivating or shaping our "relationships" with our tongues. The decline in the man's presence in the "Church House" coincides with the decline in honor being given or shown to the man. May this resource act as a catalyst to infuse change in the hearts and minds of the people.

Dr. Sybil M. Sloan

INTRODUCTION

I understand that everybody has a position they take when it comes to how a relationship should look. This book is a direct response and a clap back to *Put Your Mouth on Him* by Dr. Sybil Sloan. My endeavor is not to state that putting your mouth on him is not an appropriate means of edifying. Why? Because we need uplifting, affirming, and empowering as men from the woman or women in our lives. Women often seem to forget we have always put our mouth on the woman.

Someone is reading this saying, "how have you always put your mouth on a woman"? Just follow me through the journey of this book and you will see exactly how I have always shown a woman what she meant to me and observed how other men have always put their mouths on their women as well.

VOICE ACTIVATION

… and brought them unto Adam to see what he would call them: and whatsoever Adam called every living creature, that was the name thereof.
Genesis 2:19-20

Men, we have to understand that we have been given the power of *voice activation* and creativity. The moment Adam named or called something in creation what it was, two things happened.

> 1. ***The nature of what it was immediately was released.***
> 2. ***The purpose of what it should be was released.***

As it relates to the women in our lives whether our wife, mother, or daughter, we have to be careful of what we call them because our words release nature and purpose.

Confession

As a man I acknowledge that I was given the power to name, create, release nature, and purpose. Therefore, I must pause here before I go any further. For every woman in my life who is reading this book, please forgive me for every time that I called you anything other than a woman. This day and in this moment, I release the nature to thrive, to build, and to be creative. I also release the purpose to help, aid, assist, nurture, and bring balance to our homes, communities, nation, and ultimately our men. Let's go forth.

DADDY'S GIRL

Believe In Her

There is absolutely nothing in this world that alters a man's emotional DNA quite like the birth of his daughter. The protection we men desire to give to our wives cannot be compared to the protection we feel we must provide for our little princesses. But as our daughters grow, we must understand her need to be viewed, honored, and respected as a woman, not just Daddy's little princess.

One of the greatest gifts you can give a teenage daughter is your belief that she will be able to work things out eventually; not immediately perhaps, but eventually.

Listen To Her

After you have listened and reflected her feelings, if she is still engaged, ask her what she has already tried. Point out her creativity or courage in trying that solution, if appropriate. Find the places in her decision making of which you can applaud her. Never miss an opportunity to increase her faith in herself. Explore which aspects of her solution are working, and which are not. Ask her of her opinion of why those strategies did not work before you offer your opinion.

Often there is some part of what she has tried already that has worked- if you can find that part, you will be way ahead of the game!

Let Her Problem Solve

Now that your daughter is a teenager, she wants to solve her own problems. She thinks you can't possibly understand her problems *(in all fairness, sometimes this is actually true-the teen world has changed a lot!)* and she will be likely offended that you think you know more than she does.

Though it's hard to imagine, she actually does want your approval and even your help. It's just that what she desires to feel safe may vary from what you think she should need to feel safe. You must understand that your approval or disapproval means the world to her. She wants to know that you know you can trust her decisions.

Reassure Her

Reassure her; not so much that everything will be okay, but reassure her of the following:

1. This is exactly what the process of learning to be a mature adult looks like.

2. You(father) are confident that she will figure everything out eventually and fully be the mature, creative, and clever young adult that you see her becoming.

THE ORPHAN SPIRIT

I spent many years trying to conquer something I did not quite understand. I could not understand why my protection seemed to cause pain and why my provision incited the need to become independent in women. After studying the woman, I realized the man has been cursed, better yet challenged to show her what she has never seen.

We have oftentimes been challenged to remind her inner child that her father's absence does not negate our assignment or presence in her life, and to show her of what it feels like to have what he never made available to her.

After failed attempts, I realized it was not my pouring and depositing into her life that was being resisted. Wisdom began to show me my inability to recognize her place of pain, which caused me to create further injury to an infected area. This was important because as I felt my protection being rejected, I had begun to subconsciously not provide it at all. As I felt my provisions were unappreciated, I found other people and things to give my money to. This was my way to comfort my pain of feeling rejected.

As men, it is important that we understand every reaction from her is not towards us, even if we experience the reaction, feel the reaction, and are even blamed for the reaction. Sometimes, she may not even be conscious of the reaction, but it is up to us to know the precise moments that the little girl in our woman cries out for her father.

A COLLECTION OF PRAYERS

Do not be anxious about anything, but in everything make your requests to God ..by prayer, thanksgiving and placing your request to God, the peace of God will guard your heart and mind fully beyond understanding

Philippians 4: 6–7

Prayers for Mothers

"Lord, I just want to lift my mother up to you. Please give her Your wisdom and guide her along her path as a [*wife, mother, sister and friend*]. I ask that You'd help her by providing strength, encouraging her and guiding her as she finds balance in her life. God, I truly value her, and I pray that You'd help her be the mother and woman You'd like her to be. In Jesus' name I pray, amen."

Prayers for Mothers and Daughters

"God of Enduring Faithfulness, my mother and I have a special bond. She brought me into this world. She has protected me and loved me ever since. She has stuck with me through the good and bad of life. Please continue to nurture our relationship and build our friendship. Please make Your love the core of our relationship. Please give us faith in the journey ahead. Help us work together joyously. Amen."

A Husband's Prayer for His Wife

"When the enemy attacks her, let her faith in You protect her so that she may stand her ground. Bring your Word to her mind so that she may turn aside his assaults and fight the good fight. Help her to remember that You give us the victory through Christ *(Ephesians 6:10–18; 1 Timothy 6:12; 1 Corinthians 15:57*

Father, You loved us first—so much so that You sent Your Son to take our place. How incredible it is to think that while we were sinners, Christ died for us. Nothing we do could ever compare to the riches of Your grace."

(1 John 4:19; John 3:16; Romans 5:8; Ephesians 2:7).

"Help her to grow first in her love for You. May she be increasingly in awe of Your power, beauty, and grace. May she know more each day about the depth and width of Your love and respond with increasing love of her own."

(Psalm 27:4; Ephesians 3:18).

Prayer for Purpose

Lord, you are my maker. You fashioned me with a divine purpose in mind. Today, I yield myself and surrender to that purpose. I receive by Faith the download, revelation, and clarity of your purpose for my life.

I will cry out to God Most High, to God who will fulfill his purpose for me.
Psalm 57:2

I PUT MY MONEY WHERE MY MOUTH IS

For where your treasure is, there will your heart be also.

Matthew 6:21

This section is about just what the title reads, *I put my money where my mouth is*. What seems to be misunderstood most often, is that the mind of the woman does not always mirror the mannerisms of the man. Depending on where she has been, who has been in her life, or what male influence she is encountered; she may fail to see things from a male's perspective. Real men put their money into things that they are passionate about, care about and into the things that matter to them.

Since the beginning of time, the woman has known security and provision. The truth of the matter is that before she was brought into existence everything was in its proper order. Everything was functioning in its system and within its established cycle.

But if any provide not for his own, and especially for those of his own house, he hath denied the faith, and is worse than an infidel.
1 Timothy 5:8

Sisters, it is important that you know that you deserve verbal affirmations from the man in your life. However, please know that the words *"I love you",* are not just said, spoken, or expressed verbally; a man will put his money where his mouth is. Love is an action word. One of the greatest demonstrations of love is detailed in,

For God so loved the world, that he gave his only begotten Son, that whosoever believeth in him should not perish, but have everlasting life.
John 3:16

As a man, my way of demonstrating how I feel about a woman is often displayed by how I take care of her, tend to her needs, and how I ease her thoughts and concerns about daily living.

I am not concerned with how society thinks my placement in her life should look. I am only concerned with her understanding what my placement in life is to her. I am wanting to shower the women in my life with gifts and gratitude, that comes in one of my most valued forms, *money*. Yes, I said it, in the form of money. Where my money goes is where my heart is located.

Money is not the only way to show women you love them, but it is a way to allow them to see you are willing to give something of which you have invested sweat equity. Money is not always easy to come by, but it has always been easy for me to share it with the women in my life. If you are reading and wondering why I state *"women";* I have a daughter, a wife, and women in my family that it is my responsibility to show them *MY* way of expressing how much I care.

The truth is where a man spends his money, is where his heart is. I recommend the mouthpiece being strongly applied within the dynamics of every relationship with the prized creation called woman.

Sisters let's be sure to celebrate, honor, respect, and value the man who provides and secures the garden. Just in case you missed it, a man who is doing so is simply putting his money where his mouth is.

EFFECTIVE COMMUNICATION

Effective communication begins and ends with making sure it is love that flows through your speech and actions, and nothing else. Normal household communication should be considerate, mutually beneficial, and sweet. We learned communication in our families. But parents demanding, siblings yelling, and unnecessary fussing is not what marriage is all about.

Good communication reduces misunderstanding, keeps things simple, and makes living in close proximity joyful instead of difficult.

Be Intentional and Clear About Your Overall Intentions.

Your intention should always be to infuse happiness into your marriage. If you remember this, you will be able to consciously create happiness while at the same time avoid any hurt.

You always can say the right thing, and in the right way, if you think first. If you just blurt out how you are feeling, it won't be good. So, think before you speak or act.

Steer Clear of hurtful communications

Some people think it's humorous to tease their spouse. But people who tease generally don't take the feelings of the one they are teasing into account, or they would be very careful about what kind of teasing they do. In most cases the teased person is humiliated. They don't feel loved. Communication should be deliberate to achieve a loving result.

Try to Avoid Communicating Your frustrations

Most people typically start complaining about whatever is bothering them because its considered good to "get it all out", as if that's a form of intimacy; it isn't. Intimacy is connecting your hearts, not dumping out your personal issues; especially if you're feeling frustrated with your spouse.

Frustration is a personal reaction you can and should control. Negativity is too easy to spill into your marriage, but you should consider its effects.

Thinking your spouse should *"be there for you"* in this way and acting like a receptacle for negativity, is not marriage thinking; it is more of childish type of thinking. You need to be aware of your spouse's needs for your love. One is responsible for their own issues.

I realize sharing frustration is a big thing in the psychiatric world, but it absolutely erodes marriages. I saw it too often when I was a divorce mediator, especially for couples who went to marriage counseling first.

Learn to Communicate ideas that turn your spouse on…. I don't mean just sexually.

Get your mind off things that are troubling you. Get yourself and your spouse into a happy space. Choose this over dragging them and yourself into whatever it is that's tweaking you.

Your mind is a tool you possess. Use your free will to change your thoughts. Though not promoted as a marriage technique, controlling your own mind should be applied. It's what is called for; not venting.

LOVE FROM A HEALED MAN

One of the most misconstrued ideas about men is that men fear love. Nothing could be further from the truth. Men crave, absorb, and desire love in ways that many cannot understand. Adam, the man, was the first being to receive and give love. Adam first experienced God's love, then Adam learned to love the things God blessed him with because loving his blessings was in return still loving God.

However, it was only because Adam's healed soul was already aligned with God's love that Adam was able to easily, immediately, and naturally give that love to Eve. It must be understood that a man who is aligned with God's love speaks to his woman differently than a man who is not aligned with the love of our Creator. A man who is aligned with God knows how to allow the Godly love in him to speak to the woman in his life. His words to her will mirror what he feels is God's words to him.

You don't have to change anything about you. I love to embrace and value ALL of you.

I love how you minister to me even in the midst of my mess.

Your touch causes every part of me to rise to the occasion.

Your smile reminds me that everything is going to be alright.

I want you to live a life free of your fears.

You will never know your purpose If you continue to hold on to the pain.

I need you to stand by me, even when standing is uncomfortable, your presence gives me total assurance that all is well.

You can't quit. I know it seems like your plate is full, but I believe in you.

Your past does not matter, never again do you have to focus on who hurt you, I am here to protect you.

I love how you stare at me and cause me to drown into your luring eyes.

You are beautiful and nothing needs to change about you for me to love you.

Ever since you came into my life, nothing but great things have happened for me.

Your voice calms my raging beast.

I know that was a disappointment, but there isn't anything in life that can stop you from reaching your destiny.

I owe you a standing ovation.

I came to be YOUR Priest, Protector and Provider.

I want to give you all of me because no one else is more deserving.

You are so smart and intelligent, It is an honor to stand beside you.

When I am in your presence you make my darkness turn into light.

I apologize for not loving you how you needed to be loved.

WE ARE ONE… NO CAP

Lay your head on my pillow, I will take care of the rest.

I plan to make all of your dreams come true.

I want to rock you to sleep.

I love it when you Put Your Mouth on Me.

I am so glad you know how to effectively put your mouth on me.

I want the part of you that you have been holding back from everyone else. I want to help you be FREE.

I accept that I love you just the way that you are.

I am excited about the person you are becoming.

I forgive you for anytime that you caused me pain.

I ask you to forgive me for anytime that I have caused you pain.

You are unique. You are different in your own beautiful way.

Happiness is a choice and today I choose to be happy with you.

You are God's masterpiece.

You are a success story in the making.

You are able.

Victory belongs to you.

You are a courageous woman.

You are enough.

I decree that you possess the qualities needed to be extremely successful and influential.

You are equipped.

You are built to last.

———⁂———

You are unstoppable.

I decree that your mind is full of brilliant ideas.

I decree that you make a difference in this earth simply by existing in it.

I decree that your ability to conquer your challenges is inevitable.

You are strong.

You are ready.

Life belongs to you.

Health belongs to you.

Wealth belongs to you.

There is no failure in God.

Victory belongs to you.

The Joy of The Lord is your Strength.

---

30 DAY AFFIRMATIONAL CHALLENGE

We oftentimes minimize the power of our own words. The use of your lips to speak your security, happiness, and health is still by far your strongest ally in this war against depression, illness, and all things that do not reiterate God's voice in your life.

I challenge you for 30 days to treat your ears to the sound of you reaffirming your place in God's kingdom and on earth. It is not enough to simply read words of affirmation, the space around you needs to hear it as well. Speak the power. See the power.

DAY 1

God is My Comfort in my Tribulations

2 Corinthians 1: 3-4

3. Blessed be the God and Father of our Lord Jesus Christ, the Father of mercies and God of all comfort,

4. Who comforts us in all our tribulation, that we may be able to comfort those who are in any trouble, with the comfort with which we ourselves are comforted by God.

DAY 2

I Am Sufficient In God

2 Corinthians 3: 5

5. Not that we are sufficient of ourselves to think of anything as being from ourselves, *but* our sufficiency is from God.

DAY 3

I Will Not Fear Evil

Psalm 23: 4

4. Though I walk through the valley of the shadow of death, I will fear no evil; For you are with me; Your rod and Your staff, they comfort me.

DAY 4

My Voice Is Heard By God

Psalm 116:1-2

1. I love the Lord, because He has heard My voice and my supplications.

2. Because He has inclined His ear to me, Therefore I will call upon Him as long as I live.

DAY 5

God Is My Helper

Psalm 121: 1-2

1. I will lift up my eyes to the hills – From whence comes my help?

2. My help comes from the Lord, Who made heaven and earth.

DAY 6

I Will Not Be Moved

Psalm 125:1

1. Those who trust in the Lord are like Mount Zion, which not be moved, but abides forever.

DAY 7

God Makes Me Strong

Psalm 138:3

2. In the day when I cried out, You answered me, and made me bold with strength in my soul.

DAY 8

God Rescues Me From The Trouble

Psalm 138:7

7. Though I walk in the midst of trouble, you will revive me; You will stretch out your hand against the wrath of my enemies, and your right hand will save me.

DAY 9

God Heals My Wounds

Psalm 147: 3

3. He heals the brokenhearted and binds up their wounds.

DAY 10

My Soul Finds Joy In God.

Psalm 35: 9

9. And my soul shall be joyful in the Lord; it shall rejoice in His salvation.

DAY 11

God Will Make My Dreams Come True

In the Bible: Psalm 37: 4

4. Delight yourself also in the Lord, and he shall give you the desires of your heart

DAY 12

God Is My Strength

Psalm 37: 39

39. But the salvation of the righteous is from the Lord; He is their strength in the time of trouble.

DAY 13

My Steps are established by God.
Psalm 40: 2

2. He also brought me up out of a horrible pit, out of the miry clay, and set my feet upon a rock, and established my steps.

DAY 14

God Is Always Present In My Life
Psalm 46: 1-2

1. God is our refuge and strength, a very present help in trouble.

2. Therefore we will not fear, even though the earth be removed, and though the mountains be carried into the midst of the sea.

DAY 15

Be Still

Psalm 46: 10

10. Be still, and know that I am God.

DAY 16

I Will Trust In God

Psalm 56: 3-4

3. Whenever I am afraid, I will trust in You.
4. In God (I will praise His word), In God I have put my trust; I will not fear. What can flesh do to me?

DAY 17

My Soul Waits

Psalm 62: 5-7

5. My Soul, wait silently for God alone, for my expectation is from Him.

6. He only is my rock and my salvation; He is my defense; I shall not be moved.

7. In God is my salvation and my glory; The rock of my strength, and my refuge, is in God.

DAY 18

I Am Blessed

Ephesians 1: 3

3. Blessed be the God and Father of our Lord Jesus Christ, who has blessed us with every spiritual blessing in the heavenly places in Christ.

DAY 19

I Am Forgiven.

Ephesians 1: 7

7. In Him we have redemption through His blood, the forgiveness of sins, according to the riches of his grace.

DAY 20

My Heart and Mind Have Peace

Philippians 4: 7

7. The peace of God, which surpasses all understanding, will guard your hearts and minds through Christ Jesus.

DAY 21

I Am Chosen By God

Ephesians 1: 4

4. Just as He chose us in Him before the foundation of the world, that we should be holy and without blame before Him in love.

DAY 22

I Am Complete

Colossians 2:10

10. You are complete in Him, who is the head of all principality and power.

DAY 23

I Find Rest.

Hebrews 4: 9

9. There remains therefore a rest for the people of God.

DAY 24

I Am Strong

2 Corinthians 12: 10

10. Therefore I take pleasures in infirmities, in reproaches, in needs, in persecutions, in distresses, for Christ's sake. For when I am weak, then I am strong.

DAY 25

God Wants Me To Prosper

3 John 1:2

2. Beloved , I pray that you may prosper in all things and be in health, just as your soul prospers.

DAY 26

Trust God's Timing

Ecclesiastes 3:1

1. To everything there is a season, a time for every purpose under heaven.

DAY 27

His Timing Is Beautiful

Ecclesiastes 3:11

1. He has made everything beautiful in its time.

DAY 28

I Will Enjoy The Good of Life

Ecclesiastes 3:12-13

12. I know that nothing is better for them to rejoice, and to do good in their lives,

13. and also that every man should eat and drink and enjoy the good of all his labor – it is the gift of God.

DAY 29

I Am Loved

Isaiah 43: 4

4. Since you are precious in My sight, you have been honored, And I have loved you.

DAY 30

I Belong To God.

Isaiah 43:1

1. But now, thus says the Lord, who created you, O Jacob, And He who formed you, O Israel: Fear not, for I have redeemed you, I have called you by your name; you are mine.

IT'S OKAY TO GO DOWN ON HER

As a young adolescent, perhaps fourteen or so, I can recall having conversations with my friends of the *wills and will nots* of sex.

I must admit, I told them, *"Hey, I won't knock it until I try it"*. We have always been taught as men that we should dominate, show aggression, and lead the way. In essence of the matter, I think we should. However, I want to reveal a more perfect and natural way. According to the word, in the beginning God created us male and female. Both were equal in essence, but different in function.

It is in *that* function that we men found the underwrite of the dysfunction of or manhood. God placed man in the garden to keep it. He pulled the woman out of the man to help him keep it. With this knowledge we often feel that the woman is no more than the helper. I must say that in all actuality, woman was also created to enhance, add value, and give unique perspective.

This closing section is written to challenge the man to yield himself to essence and not just to function of a woman, because in essence we were created equal.

The female was already inside of the male, and the woman was already inside of the male before God performed anesthesia and surgery on Adam to bring Eve forth.

The word of God says,
> *"Submit ye one to another.."*
> *Ephesians 5:21*

Typically, when we see the word *submit*, to give over or yield to, we think of the word in an authoritative manner. Sir, it's okay to go down on her.

In essence she is your equal. She was pulled out of you and given to you to enhance you. When you don't humble yourself, yield to her thoughts, expressions and concerns, you actually hinder you from yourself. She is you and you are her, It's okay to go down on her.

There will be many moments in which she is definitely stronger and sharper in different areas. Sadly, many men don't welcome the leadership or dominion of the woman in those areas. Men often find themselves intimidated. Sir, she was pulled out of you to help you. Let her help you. It's okay to go down on her.

Lastly, I want to address honor. Since you have always put your mouth on her, let's take it to the next level and honor her. Let's welcome her to the garden again.

Let's not be so territorial, but instead let's give her the liberty to help us paint on the two walls of the past and the future. She is phenomenal. She was fearfully and wonderfully made. She is God's leading lady. There is so much more that she could produce if you would simply stop with the *dos and don'ts.*

She is now the vice President of your United States. What more could she become if you would just go down on her?

Sadly, at the age of 45, I'm still saying, *"Don't knock it until you try it".* Tonight is the night. It's okay to go down on her.

Let him kiss me with the kisses of his mouth: for thy love is better than wine.

Song of Solomon 1:2

For bookings, bookings, and more updates
from
Dr. Frederick Acklin
please visit

www.Dr.FrederickAcklin.com

www.ingramcontent.com/pod-product-compliance
Lightning Source LLC
Chambersburg PA
CBHW071032080526
44587CB00015B/2581